Copyright © 2022 by Julia Brooke

Classic Christmas

Stories, pictures and Christmas word puzzle games for the entire family

www.ingramcontent.com/pod-product-compliance
Lightning Source LLC
LaVergne TN
LVHW061626070526
838199LV00070B/6603